Level of YOU

BOOK OF PREPARATIONS, GROWTH, & TRANSITIONS

BREANNE ELIZABETH GUY

authorHOUSE®

AuthorHouse™
1663 Liberty Drive
Bloomington, IN 47403
www.authorhouse.com
Phone: 1 (800) 839-8640

Published by AuthorHouse 05/07/2020

ISBN: 978-1-7283-6111-6 (sc)
ISBN: 978-1-7283-6109-3 (hc)
ISBN: 978-1-7283-6110-9 (e)

Library of Congress Control Number: 2020908439

Print information available on the last page.

Any people depicted in stock imagery provided by Getty Images are models, and such images are being used for illustrative purposes only. Certain stock imagery © Getty Images.

This book is printed on acid-free paper.

CONTENTS

Preface vii

Chapter 1   A Wave of Transitions.................................... 1
Chapter 2   The Inevitable................................... 9
Chapter 3   Discipline 25
Chapter 4   Levels of Life 31
Chapter 5   Durable 47
Chapter 6   Acceptance 65
Chapter 7   Level Of You 77
Chapter 8   Understand.................................... 89

PREFACE

After it's all said and done, we get to a point in our lives where we want better. We just know there is better for us. We may even just be in a transition, or a new beginning or some sort. We see where we are and we see where it is that we want to be. We cannot fully see the challenges that we are going to face, but we are aware that there will be challenges. The thing is are we prepared for these challenges? Are we prepared mentally? Are we prepared physically? Are we prepared spiritually? Are we in control of our emotions in life? Do we have any idea of who we are this moment in time? Are we willing to undergo the consequences of our choices and decisions, should we choose the wrong ones in trying to achieve our goals in life? Are you willing to step fully and completely into the power you hold in your own life? Getting

to your level of you is not at all an easy task, but it is definitely not impossible. You are more than capable of this. You are also capable of so much more in life, that you may even be surprised.

CHAPTER 1

A Wave of Transitions

L ife itself deals heavily with growing and evolving. Such things like changes, transitions, movements and etc. There is so much beauty in it all. Growth and transitions in human beings, animals, and plants. Also in society when you look around, through inventions, the whole entire universe. Then there is even more personally the growth and transitions of one self in life. Perhaps even throughout your life, be it moving to a new city, or just trying to achieve something more in your career. Think of it all as a wave of transitions so to speak. Have you ever seen the waves in the ocean, especially at high tide and they keep moving until they reach the shore? Now compare that to your life. What if you were trying to achieve something in your life? This mostly

pertains to something big, however size doesn't matter it is the idea in the situation that needs to get across. Anyways, getting back to subject you will go through several waves of transitions before getting to your achievement yes! These transitions can be as smooth or as easy as you handle them, but they will at times have a mind of their own. Think of a surfer on a surf board, no matter if the waves or good or bad when he decides to surf he still has to be able to adjust and ride it out. Not only that he or she has to make the best of those waves, while keeping their composure and looking like a pro doing it. He or she may wipe out once or twice, or may not even wipe out at all. The only certainty there is that no matter what happens he or she will be brought back to shore. Hopefully is a safe manner. Unless something tragic happens like a shark attack, or injury. However, let us not go down that route. Let us say that all is well and he or she has arrived back to shore accomplished.

We go through transitions for a lot of reasons in life. If you really think about it growth and transitions are apart of everything in this world. A butterfly is a great example! Lots of people love butterflies. Starting off first as merely a caterpillar, and then going within its cocoon only to emerge into something truly amazing! An infant becomes a toddler, then a kid, then a teenager, then adult and so on. Plants start as seeds and grow up through the ground. Inventions evolve and transition into better things the years, generation

after generation, decade after decade. Think back to old automobiles and airplanes back then, and compare them to what they are now. Huge difference right? So if your feeling like you want to transition personally or even move to a new place in life, its more than possible. In fact its natural to feel such a way. There's so much beauty to be found in this!

You want to build, grow, and blossom in life. Your ready and wanting to achieve new things. You may even be wanting enlightenment in new areas of your life. Knowledge is power and you should definitely do so. You are fearlessly wanting to ride the wave of your transitions in life until you reach your shore. You want to get to an ultimate level in your life, your level of you. You may even need assistance or information beforehand to be as mantally prepared as possible. Well for starters, you picked the right book. Now you just have to read it and soak it all in. Your well on your way to not only find truth in yourself and the things you want in life, but to also mentally prepare you for the things that will indeed surface along the way. Transitioning may look easy from the outside, but there's so much more to it than you think. No matter what the case, it is worth it and that's all that matters. So here goes!

The main thing about transitions is that you have to allow them to fully happen. You can't cut off a transition in your life until its finished. You may get through most of it, but then leaving off even a tad bit may mean you have to start

completely over. Think of when you download something and it isn't finished and it gets disrupted. Upsetting Right? Make sure you follow through with things in your life. Not only that but if you ever feel confused in a transition its good to gain clarity before continuing. Time is important and you would not want to go through with something only to find out that wasn't really what you wanted, yet you know things were shaky going into this. Save yourself from this disappointment. Gain all the information and knowledge you can before fully committing to something and transitioning into it.

The good thing is, if all else fails in a transition you do have the option to restart at any given time. That goes for and towards anything. You should feel good about transitions that you choose. You should feel good in your transition process. If you do not, once again do take a time out and recollect.

Now since you have chosen to start your journey towards your level of you. Please and always remember the destination doesn't mean anything, if you cannot find it in you to enjoy the journey. Life is not meant to be controlled, it is meant to be handled. You should always know how to be able to adjust accordingly. Your future self will thank you for this, and it will greatly help you in succeeding to new heights by knowing how to do so.

CHAPTER 2

The Inevitable

If one thing is certain in life it is that we cannot stop the inevitable from happening. The universe and God have a way with allowing things to happen and unfold. Whether those things be good or bad there is always a reason behind this. So, what does the inevitable have to do with you getting to your level of you. A whole lot! It actually is a given advanced warning to you. You are going to run into things along your life, some that you truly hate, and some that your ever so grateful for. However, it will be those things you truly hate that will be the most important. In fact, these things will play as hidden keys to getting to your level of you. Like the saying, "sometimes you have to take a step back in order to take three steps forward." This is highly true! The thing is

you will be in much resistance to that step back. You will feel like you've failed yourself, your losing hope, your life is falling apart, perhaps you might even feel God has forgotten about you. None of these things are the case. Things can be working in your favor without you even know. That's the beauty in learning to sometimes just relax and allow the inevitable to happen.

Now there is a difference between letting the inevitable happen, and then going around and getting yourself caught up in things in life. Perhaps your even allowing bad things or horrible habits to continue. Here are some examples to help you better understand:

1) The inevitable – You lose your job and struggle to find another one for months before finding another job. Therefore, you lack money for a while, but you're truly trying to find a new job. Life right!

2) Getting caught up – You quit your job the same day you get hired at a new one. Not knowing if that's fully even the job you want, or things will work out there. You find out that is not the job you want at all after a while. You tend struggle for a while, with this bad decision that you made. You realize you now have to start over, again, and find new work. You basically just wasted a whole lot of your own time and put yourself through unnecessary trouble. This could be inevitable,

but the fact that you willingly quit a job before even knowing anything fully about the new one, or starting training is not good at all. You caught your own self up and now have to deal with the consequences of your actions. Yup, you live and learn.

All in all, you get where this is going. I guess you can say getting caught up in things are all apart of habitual behavior patterns, more than likely bad ones. The inevitable is more so things happening to you that you cannot control, nor did you fully cause. It was bound to happen sooner or later, and there is nothing you could do to escape it. So then why does the inevitable happen? Why does it exist? Why do we need it? The inevitable brings growth! You learn from it, and build, and become stronger. You become wiser and blossom into that person you've always wanted to be in life, and whatever else you always dreamt of. Think about it all. Sometimes you don't appreciate certain things in life, until you experience the downside of it. You will not appreciate great friendships until you've seen horrible ones, you will not appreciate that dream wedding and love of your life until you've seen the worst of the worst loves of your life, you will not appreciate that brand new car until you've driven in a super old one, you will not appreciate your own home or apartment until you've had to live with a bunch of people or sleep on someone's living room couch. Especially people you probably do not even like and

have to put up with noise or having your peace broken. You see the inevitable is a blessing in disguise. The phrase hard work pays of goes hand in hand with this term. This is what you need to start doing, welcome the inevitable when it comes into your life. That just means something amazing is on the rise.

So now we need to dig a little deeper, stay with me on this. There are two very special words that go with the inevitable that you will not like. People tend to avoid these words at times. One keeps us away from a lot of things we so badly want, and the other hurts our confidence and causes insecurities each time it happens. Do you know these words? Fear and rejection are the words. Yup, tough right. See these are two words you will have to learn to deal with no matter what in life, or else you will hurt your own self. Your soul, your image, your wellbeing, and all that you are will suffer if you do not learn that these words or your friends. Not your enemies, just like the word inevitable. These are help words, growth, preparation, and fruitful words. They help create you and make you all that you will be in this life.

With fear there are so many things we fear in life. That ranges from small to big. Everyone in the entire world has fears. Fear is normal. Some people like to fear, and others of us simple cannot take it and do not want to fear. Some people like scary stuff and movies, others reject such things. Perhaps, they feel as though why should we make ourselves fear when

we don't need to? Isn't life itself already scary enough? They do have a point, while others feel like they need the extra in their lives. They see it so be fun, and harmless. Then there are other fears like taking your first plane ride, moving to a new city, getting a new job where you know no one, losing loved ones, etc. Fears we must learn to overcome, and you will because it is possible. Most importantly be patient with yourself. The more you do something the less you fear it. Also have faith in yourself and what you set out to do, that things will work out and be ok.

So now it is time to take rejection! Doesn't it feel almost like it hurts just to say that word. No one likes rejection let's face it. Rejection in even the smallest things can have your whole world flipped in the blink of an eye. Having your bank card rejected at a store, really declined, but still your payment is rejected. That brings feelings of embarrassment and shame, even when you know you have money there. Perhaps you are in a different city other than a place you normally go to and fraud protection signals off. How about going for that new amazing job and you just know you nailed it because you spoke amazingly, came in well dressed, and had all the qualifications. Then you get that daunting email saying, "Dear Ms. Lianne thank you for your time, but our company has chosen to move on with someone else we thought would better suit this position. We wish you all the best and do come back again if you see another interview available soon." Ouch!

That totally sucks, it is like saying we do not want you now but if the person we chose over you lets us down we will gladly love to see you again. Then hopefully they do not reject you again since you will now be going up against new candidates. Hate to be the bearer of bad news or sound negative, but that is far from what is being done here. Truth is being shed, so at least you know what you are up against and what all comes with this type of rejection.

Now let us flip to artists. Don't we get rejection the most, it's a way of life that is imperative we learn to deal with. Everyone wants to be an artist. The ones that hit it big, hit it big! The get the fame, fortune, money, etc. It seems like everyone is constantly going at it to be the next big thing. Singers, dancers, choreographers, rappers, movie directors, entrepreneurs this list can go on and on right! Yet we struggle to deal with rejection and being told no. We let it get to us at times and break us down and destroy us and takeover of lives. Seriously, one little small word that destroys us. It shouldn't be like that at all. Rejection needs to be looked at in another light. One person no who says no is the yes of another. You must keep hope alive and keep going no matter what. Take time to be upset you have that right, but also learn to bounce back quick. Dwelling in pain and hurt might make you miss out on your upcoming yes. What a bummer that would be!

Lastly friendships and relationships, yup that too! We all want to feel wanted in life, chosen, loved by all, the life of

the party, and etc. The thing is that will not always happen. You will have people that just don't like you or don't want to be your friend the way you want them too. Like the saying," Find your tribe and love them hard." Well, newsflash you may be in the wrong tribe so move out quick. You wouldn't stay in the wrong classroom if you walked in and realized you have the wrong room number, so leave and find the right one. No one wants to feel unwanted in life anyway that's the worst feeling possible, why do that to yourself. Even in relationships. Perhaps your dating or seeing someone and not feeling it, there not putting in the effort, and then you see them showing interest in someone else. So, then you may begin to plot, scheme or whatever the case may be to try to win that person back. That's where your messed up at! Number one you need to stop, because a person treating you distant does not even deserve that type of energy or attention from you. You need to put that energy into your career and own life. Who cares if they chose someone else over you, that is a part of the inevitable let it go. Some people are only in your lives for a season, take the good and wish them well. Number three is going to be self-love, know that you deserve that absolute best so give that to yourself until someone else can.

You need to remember these three words so you don't forget, the inevitable, fear, and rejection. You must be able to handle these words before moving anywhere in life above

all things. Make your mental notes and now you should feel prepared to tackled these and better deal with them in life. You are well on your way. Keep soaking this all in, it is only the beginning.

CHAPTER 3

Discipline

I f there was no discipline whatsoever in this world there would be much chaos. Sure, there is chaos already, but it would be even worse than what we already have. We need things to keep us in line in life. Yet, there will be times when discipline is thrown out the window. There will be times when we do not even want to discipline our own selves and our behavior. We know things about us that are off the grid or need to be controlled. Yet we refuse to. Nothing is wrong with that at all. You do as you please in life. Heed you, one day something in your life will cause you to have to deal with this. To have to discipline yourself or your own actions. You may even find yourself dealing with the same things, people, and patterns over again. The problem can only be others for

so long, when are you going to stop and think perhaps, I may be out of line. The blame is different when it is placed on ourselves. We like pointing fingers until it comes back at us, then everything is a problem. Truth always reveals itself. It is something that cannot be escaped. No matter your age in life, when your forced to deal with yourself and your truth it will be very intense. It will require lots of discipline.

Did you know that your amount of success in life is also measured by the amount of discipline you have? It is true. Think of a person who cannot manage to get there rent paid, but they always spend money on other things. When the rent comes, they always have an excuse. Yet they had the rent money, they just chose to spend it on something else. Yes, we get it you want to treat yourself. However, it is the wrong time for that. Discipline yourself to handle your responsibilities first. You may even be renting out a room. I am more than sure you do not want to live there your entire life.

If we will learn to discipline anything we must discipline our feelings. We can at times let them overtake us in situations. You have to know when to turn then on and off, or at least close to. You cannot let things or people get the best of you. You cannot allow yourself to be triggered easily. Do you know even know what are your triggers? Are you aware of them?

Being triggered in the ways where you cannot control either your feelings or emotions can cause you to get into situations that often blow up! Sometimes you just got to hold

yourself for a second and step away. Take a step away and gain clarity before going overboard. Be careful of your words in heated arguments. One day you may slip and say something you cannot take back. Words do hurt people, and that hurt can last a lifetime and do damage if you are not careful. At the same time know when people do say things out of line, it sometimes has nothing at all to do with you. That is why we must learn also to keep those feelings in tack. Do not fight fire with fire. Instead show love and kindness sometimes, even when you do not understand.

Before you point fingers at another person and say to yourself this person has issues and needs to have some self-discipline, make sure you also know what you need to discipline. Easier said then done, but it is a must! As said before success requires a lot of discipline. Also make sure you are following through in life. Stopping and starting things constantly will eventually create problems. You can change things in your life, yes! Just make sure you have discipline and clear insight. Do not waste time, money, and resources constantly. Be present in your life as well. Sometimes dwelling on the past and worrying too much about the future will make you absent to what is currently happening in your life. Do not allow yourself to live blindly. Especially without reason and purpose. Without discipline there is no such thing as success.

CHAPTER 4

Levels of Life

To everything in life there is a reason, season, and order. True at times some people seem to be advancing faster than you are. Perhaps it may even seem like they have not done much at all and they just keep on accomplishing so much. That's not always the case. Yes, it can be frustrating because when you are ready for things to take off and happen, you are ready. Your patience begins to wear out and run low, you start to lose hope and give up. Do not, do not throw in the towel based off what you see others doing in life. You cannot compare yourself to the life of another, were all on different paths and journeys. You must remain focused on your own journey and gain more insight and understanding. You need to awaken yourself to truth in your own life no matter how

ugly it may be. You need to face where you are in life and the things you deal with. Wake up one day, look yourself in the mirror and be truthful with what you are seeing and feeling in life. After all it will only be you. Go wherever you have privacy to really have an honest talk with yourself. You can grow from a lie, but chances are it will not last long. The thing about lies is that you must constantly keep lying to keep it going. Eventually the truth will surface or come out. It is better to deal with it now than later down the line.

At times we are not so accepting of where we are in our lives, but that is where the real growth begins. That is where you can get to breaking lifelong habitual habits and allowing real beauty to blossom forth in your life. That is when the universe can really start better aligning amazing things for you and allow new doors to open. Think of a young boy that is a teenager, admiring an older man for where he is in life. He sees this older man as successful, having a house, nice car, great job, maybe even his own business, possibly a wife and kids. The young boy then dreams to one day be like that. He is currently leaving middle school and just getting to high school. He starts to think some nights and elaborate on the things he wants to do in life, his career path he sees himself on, how can he begin to put himself in a situation to get to these things. To accomplish the goals that he sees his admirer accomplishing. There are levels to this thing! This teenager is more than likely still living with his parents, so

for starters getting a job and beginning to save is first and foremost. He will be moving into his young adult part of his life soon. He may even be wanting to get his own apartment after high school. He may also be wanting to get his first car. His parents may help financially or maybe they will not. The thing is it is always great to make plans based off what you have and not others. If you are financially blessed in life in a way that is a bonus! Which will feel good on receiving it. Already this young man is putting himself in a great position to now save more and get to a new level of his life. In the next coming years, he will want to get another car or trade his in if it is still in great condition. Then he is probably now working a better job, with better income, and working to save for a house. He might even be thinking of starting a side hustle or having his own business one day. There aren't any limits to what you can do in life financially. Having multiple forms of income is a great benefit. Though not everyone in life can do this. Some people just really do not have the energy to handle this in life. That is ok and does not make them any less of a person. It just means that they will have to budget more, and really watch their finances extremely. Not only that, but this is not geared to just a young man in life it can also be geared to a young woman. One that is truly driven and ambitious in this case!

Next in levels, and for this do not be ashamed if this pertains to you, we sometimes as adults must start over and

get our stuff together. We may be feeling like things haven't worked out the past years as we wanted, we are not financially happy, we aren't happy in relationships, in work. We just need a miracle or a fresh beginning. You know what that is truly amazing. Age never matters in a situation too much. If you have the drive, passion, determination, and willpower that's really all you need. Even then you can still accomplish new levels in your life. This time around you may even feel happier because its better late than never. Always remember you hold the key to all things you think possible. The only way you can you lose those things is by giving that key away. Do not give it away, that's something powerful. For whoever holds your key in their hands has the power to destroy and alter your life choices and decisions. Why would you want to do something like that? Easier said than done right? Possibly!

So back to levels, wherever you are you need to be truthful with yourself and begin setting up some type of foundation. Any foundation is good to be honest, especially if you have been having terrible trouble. Let us use the example of a female who cannot save money to save her life. Everything she gets, she blows. It goes in the blink of an eye and disappears. Even she more than half the time couldn't tell you what she did with the money. She dreams big and wants an amazing life. I'm sure you see the problem in this. She needs to save, something! Even if it is five or ten dollars a week. It is a start in a new direction. It is a new level she is growing with and

on. She might get so overly happy with saving that she decides she wants a higher paying job to save even more money! Once she gets this new job, she has now succeeded in one level and is on another. You see how great and quickly this can take off, especially when you be consistent with it. Aren't you excited for this girl! Let us take this up another notch. After a few years', this woman says hey I have all this money saved and I now want to invest some of it, and profit from it. So, she turns around and does just that. Whether it's into something else or her own business. Let's say it works and she does profit heavily from it, so much to where mailbox money starts to come in. Eventually she will in time leave her job and keep this newfound thing or investments going. Maybe she won't leave her job at all. She might hit it big enough to retire for the rest of her life. The possibilities are endless when you seek new levels to your life. That was just one example to show you guys the build of this.

Sometimes you must just face yourself in order to grow. That's where the real growth and true growth happens. The lifelong growth that will do wonders for you and put you in positions beyond your wildest dreams. Even better than that, it will begin to come easier and easier as time goes on. You will begin to achieve things faster and faster. You will start to experience win after win, success after success. All because one day you decided that you wanted change in your life. You decided that you wanted to get to a new level of your life. You

believed in yourself despite what others may tell you, and despite the doubt they show towards you. Nothing matters but how you feel, because after all it is your life. You should know yourself well enough to make the right decisions for you. That is also another thing.

Who doesn't love a good saying they can connect to. You've more than likely heard, "never let your left hand know what your right hand is doing." You do not always need to announce everything to everyone in life, sometimes it is best to move in silence. The most progress is often done that way. If people already know everything you want to do or that you are going to do, they may try to hinder that to stop you from succeeding. Yes, that's horrible but that is also life. Some people are just either jealous or hateful that way. The crazy thing is a lot of them are like that and it has nothing to do with you. People like that are often upset with themselves, disappointed in their own lives, and need inner healing. So, then you must learn in getting to new levels, don't ever take it personal when people feel a certain way about you. Let them feel what they may, were all entitled to our own opinions in life. You don't even have to let them know you know how they feel towards you. Let that extra energy you feel be positive instead of negative. Then turnaround and put that into something to help and better your life. One of the best things you'll learn in advancing to new levels is that you move way faster when you don't give negative things and

people your time and energy. Always, always protect your space. Protect your energy and do not allow people to come in your life and waste time or cause problems for you. You don't deserve that by far. No one does.

It truly is an amazing feeling to see yourself get from one level to the next. It is almost as if when you first begin, you cannot even see anything. It is like I know where I want to be, but it is going to take a while. It Is going to take hard work. It will require a lot from me. Do I really have what it takes? Am I ready to see and experience massive change? Yes, you are!

Be your best motivation and root for yourself constantly in all of this. If you have ever been to a football game or a track meet, you know what stadiums are. Some of you may have even ran stadiums in a physical fitness course in school. It always gets harder the higher up you get. The beginning seems like a breeze and your strong and fearless, and then you get mid-way and realize that you must start pulling through stronger. By the time you are between mid-way and the top you feel it in your quadriceps. So, you push through as you now reach the top level. This is a great way to describe what it is like in getting to your level of you.

Lastly, we have balancing your time. Work, work, work, work, work. Yes, you must get it done. However, keep your body in good standing. Be good to your body, you only have one. Make time for self-care, make time to be social and attend events, and make time for the people you love. Not

knowing how to balance your time along the way of your journey, can leave you feeling not so good. It can wear you down mentally and throw you off. You must really listen to your body and what it needs daily. Maybe you said on Tuesday I will do x, y, and z. Then Tuesday comes and you realize I need this to be a self-care day. I need time to myself, I feel a little sleepy or worn down. Taking that time does not mean you are lazy and no good. If you still take care of those things you put aside, you will be fine! The self and body always know what it wants and needs. It is up to us to listen! If you fail to you will be forced to sooner or later.

CHAPTER 5

Durable

H ope you now feel somewhat ready to take on something new in your life or tackle a list of things you need done in the next coming months and years. Know that you are getting yourself ready for the long haul, that you are now setting out to conquer your levels of life. Know it won't be easy, and what's easy won't be worth it. Take pride in the fact that already you see yourself as fit for the job. You know that no matter what your choosing not to give up and go into this thing fully armed. Whatever being fully armed may look like to you. When the going gets tough you will ride your waves accordingly. You have now left shore and you are out there in the middle of the ocean with your surfboard. This act of diving in, is an accomplishment.

Sometimes people do not acknowledge the fact that they must take breaks when necessary. What good is producing material and working amid you being fully burnt out. Nothing too good will come from that. I am more than sure several of us have done this. Do not torture yourself. Know when to push through and when take a break. Taking a break does not mean you are giving up. In fact, it is sometimes necessary. You do need to refresh, regain strength, and see the bigger picture. You may also need to step back and see what has been working and what has not. Perhaps you need to change up some things in life. Maybe habitually you have been doing things that's just not making the cut for you. That is not at all bad, that is good. You are inviting and allowing your take a step back phase to happen. Wait until you see the benefit from it. This is also something a lot of people don't want to accept. Things will stay shaky until you are forced to have to do this. No matter what way it comes about, you will experience much happiness and growing from this. Especially when you see yourself advancing further and at a much faster peace. Know that no matter how things may seem to look, you are always in control. Whether you think you are or not.

Hopefully before you begin your level climb you have already understood the importance of preparation. If not, it is okay because some people still do not, and others rather do without it. Though preparation is very important it can make or break you. The down fault in being broken is that

some people don't bounce back from it. Being broken can mean a lot of things from small to major. Some people luck out by the grace of God and always manage to get out of being into broken situations. That is great, but do not always count on lucking out! Here are some things you should know. Financially you should aim to always be two to three months ahead on rent. If you are just doing so awesome and amazing you may aim to be three to four months ahead on rent. You should always have some type of savings money or emergency money. You should not make huge purchases unless you have two to three times that amount in your account. Sometimes you just must suck it up and wait. Say you need a new laptop, but you do not have the money now. You may have to make trips to the library occasionally until you can save to get one and gladly do your work in the comfort of your own home. You may need a new car, but it is better to take public transportation and save up more than it will cost you just in case something happens to it. Avoid repeats in life, those aren't good feelings. No one wants to experience the same thing over twice, and not a third time. The quicker you learn lessons and move on, the faster you reach new levels in life. Don't be ashamed to ask for help either. Yes, we at times just want to get things done on our own. However, if someone offers help along the way be open to it. Allow some of that weight to fall off your shoulders, you may just deserve it. All in all, understand

that preparation is very important. Don't set yourself up for failure. Set yourself up for success!

In being durable throughout all of this you want to be built to last! Along the way in your levels of life as an artist, dancer, choreographer, rapper, businessman or woman, etc. You will need things to help you propel forward. Things such as technology, tools, media, working supplies. Whatever the case may be know that you are your greatest investment. You should always carry yourself in a good and professional manner! If you want the best, go and get the best. If you need something temporary until you reach a new level and your able to get what is permanent, do whatever works for you. Let us look into this more. Nothing is wrong with buying cheap things, it saves money. You may even luck out and get something that works or has a quality that's just as good as the expensive item. It is indeed however worth it to save up and buy the product that is more expensive and has a better quality. It will last you longer in your career and be so worth it! You may even take better care of it, because you not only love it but realize the amount of money put into it. The cheaper product even though the quality may be the same it might not endure as long. This means that you will have to keep buying it repeatedly. This after a while will come to the price of the expensive item, if not more. It pays to wait and be patient sometimes.

You will eventually learn to invest in things that are

worth it and get what last longer, even if it takes you a while. Whatever you choose to do, please be smart about it.

So, you have everything you need or perhaps just about. The thing is even when you think you have everything you need, as you grow and build and get to new levels that will change. You will start to need other things and may even want to advance your old things. Anyway, your starting your building process, your climb, your main journey. If you're still seeing this as that surfer out in the open water, you are now about to stand up on your board because the waves are coming. How exciting this is!

If you must know anything, know this. You may not see progress every day, but every so often you will. You dream at night about how it would feel to finally get to the highest of high levels in your life. Will things turn out how you expected? Will you be rerouted somehow, and it turns out different? Will things turn out much worse than expected? Will things turn out better than expected? Well, don't overthink. Learn to trust the process and just roll with it!

The main thing is to pace yourself now that it has all began. Move steadily yet take your time. Reward yourself for the little accomplishments along the way. Watch how you begin to move and rise in your climbing process. Sometimes even achieving levels without notice. Yes, after a while it can be that smooth! Do not forget if you get or feel stuck you can always call out for help. If you feel there is no one to call out

for help from, go within and re-work things. There is always a solution to a problem. Even if that solution is one you don't like. Doing what's right is not always easy, and what is easy is not always right. Remember slow and steady is always better than racing and rushed. What is the fun in hurrying to get something done. You know once it is done, its done! There may not be anything more after that. However, in taking your time, you may learn new things, have new experiences, and even new ideas come forth. This will in turn draw expansion into your life. Not only will you reach your level of you, but you will bring in and gain access to infinite levels. It pays to be patient and have faith in yourself, it really does.

So, support during those times you need to be durable, and build. Having support means a lot in anything in life. It makes you feel happier, feel lively, loved, cared about, it drives you, and creates even more passion. Having the right support fuels your success! That's why it is important to have support systems. Not only that but make sure you have the right people in your support system. You have the power to pick and choose these people, make sure you choose wisely.

Lastly in this chapter we will mention the reward system. It's so important to self-reward yourself in your climb to new levels. People aren't always going to clap for you every step of the way. Do not always seek for validation from others. It will only leave you feeling let down. The only validation that matters is yours. Not saying so to speak disregard everyone

and the way they feel about you and how your living your life. You do know what is best for your life now. People don't always know what is really going on from the outside looking in. Some days you will have to pat your own self on the back, clap for yourself, and be your own motivation. In time hopefully others around you, friends, family members, and colleagues will awaken to see what it is you are doing and your progress. Then they will start to show their happiness for you and support. In the beginning it can be really challenging when you are just beginning on this new path and realizing that you're ready to level up and build, that you're ready to sore and fully prosper!

Have you ever heard a person tell you that people aren't with your movement until they see it moving? Doesn't that sound harsh? It is highly true though. Nope you don't always need to have everything moving all the time, and full blown into effect for people to believe in you. It would help though, all the way. Understand things take time in life. You may have a couple people watching and noticing but just waiting for more to happen. You may even decide you want to wait it out until everything is completely done before releasing anything. Once again, whatever floats your boat.

Now be extremely cautious on this. Can we shed some light on something? This is important and something you should always keep in mind. We've all heard of the story with the little hen who made the bread and asked for help in the

beginning and no one wanted to help. Upon finishing those who were asked to help, smelled the bread and came in the kitchen and you know the rest. You see where this is going. Let's first say always have love in your heart, and never bow down to treating others like they treat you. Especially if you have been treated in rude manners, disrespected, the whole nine yards. Always be the bigger person. Class and grace always win the race! Getting back on subject know there is a difference in people who pay attention and clap for you and motivate you at times or down the line. Then there is a difference in those who do nothing at all, and when it's all said and done they show up clapping at the front line. You know what you do, show them love but at a distance. You don't even have to make it known how you may truly feel. You just let it go and move on with your life. Guilt is a heavy weight that no one wants to carry around in life, and that they will truly feel. Without you even having to do anything. So, do not you ever worry, cry, pain, hurt or anything when people do not show you the love and respect your desires. That says nothing at all about you but a whole about them. Always motivate and reward yourself first, and the real ones will come around and do the rest!

Also know that when you decide to take on something in your life, anything, especially in building your career. You are responsible to fund it. It is nobody's job to give you money for all your hopes and dreams. That is not how life works. You

work for the things you want. Along the way if your blessed with money from wherever be thankful and grateful for that. So do not go around thinking people owe you this and that, because they do not. Especially if you are a grown adult. Handle your business in life! Know when to fund things or invest in yourself, and when not to.

CHAPTER 6

Acceptance

You are getting along fine in conquering new levels in your life. You may have dealt with some things along the way, you may not have. Your seeing things that work, things that don't work, and things that need some adjusting. You are now having growth in recognition of situations. You are at a stage where your more awakened to acceptance. A lot of times this happens along the mid-way of getting to our level of you. You look back and see all that you've accomplished and overcame. You realize where your currently at, and you now have an estimation of how long it may take you to get to where you need to be. It might not be fully right but trust me you will kind of know. You will feel it mostly within your heart, mind, body, soul, and spirit.

You begin to sense new winds of change, and welcome new waves and beginnings. Next thing you know self-evaluation begins to kick in heavily. This is without a doubt the most mind blowing, yet beautiful part of your journey. Your climb of levels and all, your now fully awakened to all that is within you and seeing things for what they are. No longer allowing yourself to be blinded by anything and anyone. You shouldn't anyway. You owe it to yourself to see truth now in all situations and everyone in your life. Your now done with games, your done with anything that has no real concern or regards to yourself whatsoever. No, its not being mean, it is being honest and respectful. Respectful to yourself enough to know that you refuse to put up with any nonsense that will prohibit you from getting where you need to be. You will not only rise above it, but you will see above it! You will accomplish getting to a level of such peace and happiness, that it will feel like those things or people that once bothered you are irrelevant. You will know without a doubt once you reach such a place. People look at acceptance as something hard to deal with and come to terms with too. Yet you will find it is one of the most freeing and liberating things you can do for yourself in life, here is why!

Self-love is why! If you cannot accept yourself why should others. Even if you already do love yourself, love yourself even more. Love yourself so much people think that your obsessed, and they may even start to question whether they even love

themselves enough. The journey within, and of self-love will leave you glowing the brightest ever. We should always have self-love whether were single or in a relationship. Self-love during your single season in life shows you how to not only better care for yourself, but how you would like to care for your future partner or spouse. It is very enlightening. You see things you do like and don't like. You see areas of your life where you have it all together and areas where your like, I need huge improvement here. Everyone should experience this in life, no doubt about it! In acceptance, moving on from self-love we have two more important words that bring out the light in this above all. Some of us will not get to fully love our selves unless we deal with these words. Meet the words dealing and healing. Tough! Well not for all, but some yes. In life we tend to avoid things or sweep them under the rug and hope no one notices. Just like a lie eventually the truth will surface and when it does truth hurts. It hurts even deeper when you keep covering it up with lies. So, let us touch dealing and healing now.

When it comes to dealing with things we tend to dismiss it. The day you decide to face yourself in the mirror you may be afraid of what you will see. So, you rather not look in the mirror. You may be accustomed to living a certain type of life, even though you are stuck, you are afraid of change. You may not at all even be willing to move to new levels, despite feeling ready.

Why do we not want to deal with things in our life? Why do we run from things in our lives? What does this have to do with accepting ourselves.

Well your willing to move to new levels of your life, but not feeling ready because you need to face yourself. Once you decide to do that it will require dealing with yourself. It will require you stop running from things, people, places, and situations. It will require you to face the facts no matter how harsh they may be. Things about yourself that you need to change and own up to. You will have to go within and dig deeper, so deep it will make you uncomfortable. What you fail to realize is so much growth happens outside of your comfort zone. Let that uneasiness sink in and consume you. Let it transform you from the inside out. You will now advance from dealing to healing. Which is exactly where you need to be.

You see we are born with certain traits in life made from our DNA, and others we inhabit as we grow up. More than likely from the environment where always around. You might not want to face yourself in the mirror because you feel ugly. You didn't come out of the womb feeling ugly. Who told you that you were ugly? Who made you feel that way? What environment has made you become drawn to the conclusion that beauty is not something you possess. You may not want to deal with that fact, see, or own up to be an angry person. Why are you so angry? In what way has life triggered you?

You see there's so much more to the reasons of us feeling a certain way about ourselves and others. We must learn to deal and heal in this life. Especially in getting to your level of you. You cannot take old ways and habits to help you advance to new levels if they are not currently working for you.

Change is not something to be constantly feared. There will be several stages of your life that you go through, and in some or if not one you will seek some type of change. Change is natural. Stepping into new or unknown chapters of your life holds the key to new birth. Being smart about things, and using your resources wisely is the key to acceleration. Make the choice to be better and do better. Make the choice to deal and heal for your own sake.

Healing throughout your climb, build, and journey to new levels can mean a lot of things. Healing from past traumas, healing from bad friendships, bad relationships, career failures, accidents physically, the limits are endless. Healing can be from the smallest things to the biggest things. The toughest things to heal from are the things that we as humans either refuse to see or were blind to it. The thing is it's something that must be done. Every new level of your life will require a new you. By the time you get mid-way through your journey of levels, the old you will have faded. The new you will now be surfacing. By the time you near your height of all heights, you won't even remember the old you.

Healing is a great way to better learn and understand

yourself, it really is. You will begin to see things and understand things you did not before. After a while you will be able to fully see if certain issues or really coming from others, or are they coming from you. The issues that are coming from others you will learn how to better understand and deal with them, in such a way those issues no longer exist. When it comes to emotional healing it can seem like the hardest thing to do, simply because at times emotions just happen. Were human, we feel. The thing is you will eventually have to learn how to gain control of those emotions. Think if everybody in this world just acted off impulse and emotions. This would not be a peaceful world at all, not saying that it fully is now. However, it would be way more violent. Think of all the people that would be constantly hurt and torn down. All because you cannot gain control of your emotions. Sometimes things just happen and slip out but doesn't mean it has to stay that way. If you lose your temper on someone and get upset, what good would it be to stay mad with them the rest of your life? It takes more energy out of you to be negative than it does to be positive. Use your energy wisely.

So hopefully you get it, you need to deal and heal. That is major key in this acceptance process. It will however take time and won't be to pretty in the beginning. It will be worth it though. It will be life changing, and it will begin to be fun after a while. What you once seen as uncomfortable and an uneasy process, you will now see as a transforming and enlightening process.

CHAPTER 7

Level Of You

A s you keep going on your climb and journey, things
will begin to come at ease. You will now begin to gain
full recognition of all things surrounding you. You
will no longer be blinded in your environments, and naïve to
things. You will now see things for what they truly are and
won't even make excuses about them. Truth, organization,
and priorities are things you will be constantly drawn to in
your life. You just know your getting even closer and closer
to your level of you. Things now feel open and inviting for
you, when they once felt closed off and difficult. You will
breathe in new air and new beginnings all the time. You will
walk, talk, act, and now think differently. Things that use
to draw in your interest, you will no longer have any mind

space for. You have now acquired so much. You are also ready to embark on infinite levels once you reach where you have longed to be at.

You are finally breaking through! Make sure your breakthrough is with style, class, and ease. It seems like breakthrough is something that feels impossible a bit upon beginning, but then mid-way through you believe more. Even if things seem so far away. You have seen progression, so it gives you something to have hope and faith in. When that breakthrough finally comes it will all happen so fast you may not even believe it at first. Believe it! You did the necessary work, you put in the time and energy, you dug deep even when the going got tough, you made sacrifices constantly even when you really weren't able to, you proved to yourself that your worthy, you accomplished things constantly, you were patient with yourself however long you had to be, and you got to your level of you! This first breakthrough is just the icing on the cake. Those infinite levels after that will make it that much better. Think if it as the extra decorations that make the cake dazzling times ten. The sprinkles, extra colored icing, writing perhaps, added towers, sparklers, confetti, candles, figurines. See how amazing this gets! A breakthrough you have waited for so long, finally achieved!

So now that you've made it where you want to be, if you have been gaining more of yourself and talents along the way you will experience infinite levels. You will continue to build

on top of what is already built or achieved. In such a way that it's almost as if those things were already in line to happen for you. It's like a dancer that sets out on a journey to pursue this ultimate dance career, that just so happens to sing. Along the way of one journey she advances her singing. Then on top of that, she may find that she is amazing in doing hair. She then starts a side hustle doing hair. She may even be pursuing dancing, while doing hair on the side, and training for singing more. Then she starts getting booked in both dancing and singing gigs. Things have a way of working themselves out for you, without you even knowing at times. She might even be in pursuit of dance and becomes this world-renowned hair stylist! You cannot close yourself up to your gifts and talents. You need to really be more open to them, and more open to finding out exactly what it is you love to do. What makes you smile? What makes your soul happy? What makes you so passionate to wake up and do every day? What keeps you going despite turmoil in the world? What would keep you going even if you lost everything you had? What would inspire you to turn around and get it all back again?

It even goes beyond just being infinite levels. You now welcome in infinite abundance and prosperity. What a huge blessing that is! You can do anything you put your mind to. Always remember to trust in yourself, and your guidance within. Even if it may lead you astray at times. Being led astray can be a blessing in disguise. You may not understand

it as it's happening, but further down the line you will. Which will make you that much more thankful for those things that happened.

Celebrate good times! You should celebrate your success! Other people should celebrate it to, but do not be looking for it. Do not have expectations in regard to certain things and situations too much. Allow things to happen on its own.

More than likely you'll tend to look back, you'll want to recap certain things. You will take into consideration the good, bad, memories, triumphant, and tribulations along the way. Nothing is wrong with looking back, but don't look back too long. Do not allow yourself to get drawn too much to your past life. Not only that always remember to be fully present in your present life. It happens to the best of us. You can be in a present situation, but mentally somewhere else. Don't do that to yourself. Also, in getting to new levels you won't fully be able to. As you start to go higher and higher it will require that you mentally move on from things. At first it may be difficult start this process. As time goes on it will get quicker and quicker to be able to do. Be thankful for how far you've come and give yourself a pat on the back. Also give credit where credit is due. We will elaborate more on that in the final chapter, which is the next chapter.

When it is all said and done you need to ask yourself would you do it again? If you had to start all over in this level process would you gladly go back to your starting point

and begin the climb? Most people would probably say no, no way! Never again! Who would want to redo something such as an entire process of going through your life and having to figure so much out and strive to get where you want to be. Some people might just have enjoyed it that much that they would do it again. Regardless of the answer you need to always remember one thing. You only get one life, and one life only. It is imperative that you do not waste your time or procrastinate. You want to get something done, do it right away! Stop putting things that are dear to your heart and soul on hold. Sure, it takes things time to build. However, get started on those things, make moves, and do not be afraid to step out on your own. Before you can trust in anybody you have to learn to trust in yourself. Also know that you have a divine right to change at any given time, what you want to pursue. Perhaps growing up you wanted to pursue a career in one thing, and later down the line you decide that is no longer where your passion lies. That is okay, that is beautiful, and that is you understanding what really sets your soul on fire. Just like we talked about in the infinite levels. You may have several things that set fire to your soul when its all said and done. You don't have to let any of them go. The thing is one will have more importance to you than the other. So, its your own personal climb, story, journey, and accomplishment in levels. What that means to you will forever be etched in your memory. Even if you look back and recap a road or climb that

was tough, risky, and quite gruesome. If you find that it was worth it without a doubt, that is all that should matter in the end. Beauty comes from ashes. From ashes a phoenix rises!

You will know without a doubt when you have arrived at your greatest level in life. What an amazing moment in time that will be to you to always remember. To know that you did what you set out to do. To know you made it and it all began with a single choice, to want to do better and want change. You should be immensely proud of yourself no matter what anyone tells you. You will find much happiness at this height.

CHAPTER 8

Understand

So, not to bust your bubble after telling you about your level of you, but there are some things that you need to understand. This book is a mental preparation guidebook in helping you move and advance to new levels of your life. It can mentally help you as much as it wants to, but you must be willing to do the work and make the changes here. This is about you and it begins with you. This is not for the mentally weak. Even those with strong minds, still slip up and fall off track. However, your mindset can be strengthened through this. By choosing to step out onto a new journey in life and climb to new heights is already your first accomplishment, and a major accomplishment at that.

Even just simply reading this book is an accomplishment as well.

We have talked a lot and covered so many things. This next one may really get to you, and if it does that is ok. It is supposed to. Despite everything you go through, the good, the bad, the ugly, you need to always find happiness in it. In your lowest moments will be some of the greatest times of your life in this journey and process of leveling up. Do not try to avoid these times, for this is when you gain the most strength. Emotions can also run wild at times, even some you will not understand. That is ok as well, just do not beat yourself up about things. Always remember that once again you cannot control life, but you can control yourself. If you struggle to control your emotions work on that, heal if you need. At some point in time you will have to, especially in order to oversee you. This life will test you in a hundred and one ways, and if you let it get the best of you and overtake you that is it! Some things you cannot bounce back from at all! Sometimes second chances, turn into no more chances quick! When you're on a roll, stay on a roll. You may get off and mess it up, and it might not be as easy to get it rolling again.

One of the biggest obstacles people face in life is being alone. No one likes to be alone or better yet feel alone. You must get over that quick. Yes, it may get depressing at times. Even more so when your going through so much in this process and you feel so much weight. You may even feel like

no one understands what you are going through, and no one even cares. Well first off no one knows, if you have not already told anyone. If you do decide to share things in your life, make sure it is with a trusted friend. Everyone should have a trusted friend to confide in, in this life. You will have times where you do need to vent. Keeping things bottled up all the time only can hurt you in the long run. Even worse it will turn into something you may not have intend once it is finally released. So ok you may not like the alone parts of this. Let us change this into a positive. Alone time is where you also can truly transform if you allow it. All attention is on you, you can see clearly, you can think much clearer. You will be better able to sort out things in your life and see what makes since and what does not. See if you really still want to do A and B, or should you now do A and C? Those of you who love to make plans in your organizer, or perhaps make advanced plans. Are you moving too fast? Should you pace yourself more? Is everything your trying to do really have importance? Remember you need time for yourself to, and social life. Always have balance, without it you can sometimes feel your world crashing.

This life will not always be easy, but it will be what we make of it. Make everything count, every moment, every second, every minute, every week, every month, and every year. It is crazy at times how your whole life can change on

the blink of an eye. Sometimes for better and sometimes for worse. How we handle it is all up to us.

Lastly before you put this book down and set off into this world to do whatever it is your taking on. You must know this. Live in your truth always! It is lots of fun to pick up on things that others are doing in life, and nothing is wrong with that. However, you must make a voice for yourself. If you base your life off another person's eventually the facade will begin to fade. Once it falls you will be left trying to latch on to something or someone else. You will feel stuck and confused, even worse frantic at the fact that you do not even know what to do next. Stop now while you can, in order to save your own self. Find your truth and your calling. Use the things God has given you to your advantage. You can always add to that yes but remain to your truth! If you do not know or you are unsure pray about it. Pay attention to things you do daily, follow the signs in your life until it is made clear. The crazy thing is we spend our whole lives searching for things that are already inside of us. Take your blind fold off, and open your eyes, open your heart, and open your soul to your own self. Acknowledge it and cherish it. Give yourself the okay to be true to you and fully bloom into the person you were always meant to be in life. You deserve that much. Goodluck on all your endeavors in life!

Printed in the United States
By Bookmasters